BECOME A
PROFITABLE
T-Shirtpreneur

BECOME A
PROFITABLE
T-Shirtpreneur

SHANKAR HEMRAJANI

Worldwide Published by
Pendown Press

PENDOWN PRESS
An ISO 9001 & ISO 14001 Certified Co.,
Regd. Office: 2525/193, 1st Floor, Onkar Nagar-A,
Tri Nagar, Delhi-110035
Ph.: 09350849407, 09312235086
E-mail: info@pendownpress.com
Branch Office: 1A/2A, 20, Hari Sadan, Ansari Road,
Daryaganj, New Delhi-110002
Ph.: 011-45794768
Website: PendownPress.com

First Edition: 2023

ISBN: 978-93-5554-491-9

All Rights Reserved
All the ideas and thoughts in this book are given by the author and he is responsible for the treatise, facts and dialogues used in this book. He is also responsible for the used pictures and the permission to use them in this book. Copyright of this book is reserved with the author. The publisher does not have any responsibility for the above-mentioned matters. No part of this publication may be reproduced, distributed, or transmitted in any form or by any means, including photocopying, recording, or other electronic or mechanical methods, without the prior written permission of the publisher and author.

Layout and Cover Designed by Pendown Graphics Team
Printed and Bound in India by Thomson Press India Ltd.

My Dedication

With immense gratitude, I honor my guiding star, Gurudev Sri Sri Ravi Shankar Ji, whose wisdom and light continually illuminate my path.

I dedicate this book to him as he transformed my life and helped me discover my real self. I will be forever indebted to him.

Contents

Preface	1
Acknowledgements	3
Foreword *Ranjiv Ramchandani*	5
Foreword *Mangal Kothari*	6
Why This Book ?	7
Know About Me!	8
My Vision	10
Our Story-The Humble Beginnings Towards Entrepreneurship	11
Who Should Read This Book?	14
Our Milestones	15
Decoding the Challenges Faced By Small Fashion Retailers	17
Deconstructing The Retail Code	22
– Introduction to Retail Management	
– Retail Business Model Canvas	
– Retail Mathematics	
Future of T-Shirt Industry	24
– Overview	

- The Indian Market
- The Growth Drivers
- Price Points
- Preferred Fabrics
- Top Trends

Profitability Hacks For Aspiring And Established T-Shirtpreneurs 29
- Hack #1
- Hack #2
- Hack #3
- Hack #4
- Hack #5
- Hack #6
- Hack #7

Working Towards Your Health & Wellness 51

My Recommendations For Wellness Courses 54

Recommendation For Meal Routine For Retailers 58

Testimonials 61

Conclusion 64

Heartfelt Gratitude For Readers 65

Let's Connect... 66

Preface

Are you into the fashion retail business? Want to know how to become a successful entrepreneur in T-Shirt retailing? If you are reading this book, chances are you have a passion for fashion and want to start your own T-Shirt retail business. You may have already taken the first steps towards entrepreneurship or are considering it for the first time. Whatever your situation, this book is here to guide you through the process of starting and growing a successful T-Shirt retailing business.

Starting a T-Shirt retail business can be a challenging but rewarding endeavor. The fashion industry is constantly evolving. It can be difficult to keep up with the latest trends and market demands. However, anyone can succeed in the T-Shirt retailing industry with the right strategies and tactics.

This book is designed to provide you with practical advice and actionable steps that you can take to start and grow a successful T-Shirt retailing business. We have included real-life examples and case studies from successful T-Shirt retailers to illustrate the concepts and strategies presented in this book.

Whether you are just starting or have been in the industry for a while, this book will provide the knowledge and skills needed to succeed in T-Shirt retailing. We hope that by the end of this book, you will be equipped with the tools and resources necessary to launch your successful T-Shirt retailing business.

Thank you for choosing "Become a Profitable T-Shirtpreneur". We wish you all the best in your entrepreneurial journey!

Acknowledgements

Writing this book has been no less than a journey for me. I sailed through it smoothly reliving my entire journey of life till date and eventually trying to create an impact in the life of my readers through this book. But, honestly, this book would have not been possible without the love and support of my near and dear ones.

Firstly, my most important pillars of support - My parents. It is their unconditional love, support and blessings that kept me going while writing this book. Next, I would extend my heartfelt gratitude to my life partner, my wife who has always been there in the highs and lows of my life. She has been a guiding force for me as she helped me in building a successful business as well as in writing this book. I would also thank my daughter who also supported and motivated me in accomplishing this task.

A special mention for my mentors Mr. Rahul Jain and Mr. Jagmohan Singh whose teachings helped me in establishing a successful business. I would also like to express my immense gratitude to my business partners, whose guidance and expertise have played a key role in getting me here. Without their commitment, none of this would have been possible. I know that the relationships established between us early on will guide us through future successes. Words can't express my gratitude for their ongoing help and support throughout this endeavor.

It would be my honor to thank Mr. Dinesh Verma, CEO- Pendown Press without whom this book would not have been accomplished. He guided me throughout the journey of planning, drafting, writing and eventually publishing this book.

Lastly, a special thanks to every force present in the Universe for helping me transform this dream into reality. I wish to do justice with this book and help as many readers as I can.

Foreword

For me, it evokes the names of two musicians I highly respect: The first one is, Ravi Shanker, for taking Indian music to the West and second one is L. Shanker, the manic genius of the Mahavishnu Orchestra.

And then there is 'Shanker' Hemrajani. The business entrepreneur(or shall I say the tshirt tycoon), from Jaipur.

Shanker understands 'tshirt art', the raison d'et of the tshirt business, or graphic communication on a tee, along with the brand promise that it brings with it.

But more importantly, Shanker brings retail acumen, and the critical last mile coverage every brand needs, to succeed.

This book will explain to the budding entrepreneur the nuts and bolts of the business, from brand conceptualism to ultimate sale. Shanker and his team are still putting his plans in place, even as you are reading this.

Here's wishing him and his team continued success in his endeavors!

~Ranjiv Ramchandani
Founder, Tantra tshirts

Foreword

It is very nice that Shri Shankar Hemrajani has come out with a Book for Aspiring & Established T-Shirtpreneurs.

The good part is that Mr. Shankar has shared his thoughts from a personal self-experience of an Aspiring T-Shirtpreneurs to an established one. So all the inputs are very practical and implementable.

T-Shirt is a product that touches everyone's life from a small child to grandparent. So T-Shirtpreneurs will mushroom in every corner of the world.

This book will certainly be a guiding light for many entrepreneurs to establish themselves as T-Shirtpreneurs.

I congratulate Mr. Shankar for this unique first-of-its-kind initiative in the world.

Thank You & good wishes to all T-Shirtpreneurs.

~**Mangal Kothari**
Founder and Director
Offbeat Apparels India Pvt. Ltd.

Why This Book?

Way back, when I started my entrepreneurial journey, I had no guidance or information as to how I would pave my path and build a successful business as a T-Shirtpreneur. I used to wonder, how I wish I had some knowledge book or mentor or a guide that could teach me the fundamentals of this business. But, as we all know, experience is the biggest teacher in our life. I learnt from my failures and succeeded in building a successful business in the form of 'The T-Shirt Shop'.

Today, when I see young enthusiastic people being passionate about this industry, I feel like extending my help and support to them. This book is for individuals passionate about heading their retail fashion business and emerging as an established T-Shirtpreneur. This book will educate the retailers about the tactics of new age T-Shirt retailing. It will highlight upon the importance of specialized retailing in today's scenario considering the niche clarity. The book covers and narrates about the importance of automation that can help you in running your retail business in an auto-pilot mode.

Know About Me!

Hello Readers,

Firstly, thanks for stopping by and reading this book.

Hi, my name is Shankar Hemrajani and I am an MBA turned next generation entrepreneur. I come with an enriching experience of more than a decade in the T-Shirt Business. Being a spiritually grounded minimalist, I am on a mission to redefine our fashion retail industry and employment system by creating a new breed of T-Shirtpreneurs. Ever since, I succeeded in developing a scalable business model in the form of 'The T-Shirt Shop', I have been helping aspiring entrepreneurs who are keen to run a profitable T-Shirt business. We started The T-Shirt Shop in 2015. Today, by the grace of God and with the help of a supportive business ecosystem, we have succeeded in having our company stores as well as franchise stores.

It is rightly said that, 'All efforts lead to new inventions.' When I started, I never thought this concept would become a new-age franchise model retailing concept. From humble beginnings, it has now become something that can work anywhere - from high streets and malls to airports and highways. Through extensive research, testing and development of different formats, we have created a system that works well in stores from as small as 100 sq ft to 800 sq ft. This is an innovative achievement that will no doubt continue to thrive for many years to come.

I believe that every person has a unique talent and should be given the right opportunity to make the maximum use of their talents and skills by harnessing them into something big.

I firmly believe that entrepreneurship is not just about starting something new; it's about making something bigger than you ever thought possible. It's about creating something that will change lives and create value for yourself and others around you!

I thank my team, suppliers, customers, vendors, channel partners and franchises for helping me earn a name in the T-Shirt Retailing industry and referring me ahead confidently.

My Vision

The vision of The T-Shirt Shop is to become the leading provider of high-quality, stylish and affordable t-shirts that customers love to wear. We strive to offer a wide selection of designs that cater to different tastes and preferences, while maintaining the highest standards of quality and customer service. Our ultimate goal is to create a loyal customer base that trusts us to consistently deliver exceptional products and experiences, and to make a positive impact on the world by promoting sustainable and ethical practices in our operations.

Our Story - The Humble Beginnings Towards Entrepreneurship

My journey as an entrepreneur began way back in 2008 after a few years of completing my MBA, when I decided to pursue my passion for starting a business from scratch rather than joining my father's well-established enterprise. But, before that, I sought out a learning opportunity and took on the role of Assistant Sales Manager at Morarka Organic Food Pvt Ltd. At Morarka Organic, I gained invaluable knowledge about sales, marketing, operations, and other business concepts, while developing a new vertical related to their organic food range.

With a newfound understanding of business operations, I decided to pursue my entrepreneurial dreams and added a new vertical to my father's business, specializing in the export of fresh fruits and vegetables. I was able to generate export orders from one of the leading departmental stores in Dubai called Choithrams. Then I got an order for exporting mangoes to the USA from another customer. Unfortunately, the recession hit and we incurred significant losses, leading to the closure of the business.

Undeterred, I then started importing and selling yoga mats to the local yoga community, but this venture also proved unsuccessful. At a loss for what to do next, I had two options - either join my father's business or take a last chance with a capital-light model. This was around 2008.

Fortunately, I stumbled upon an opportunity to take on a franchise of a T-Shirt brand called Tantra, which eventually became the foundation for my successful retail brand.

Despite facing initial skepticism from naysayers who believed that an only T-Shirt shop would not survive, I have been fortunate enough to run that outlet successfully by focusing on providing great customer service and utilizing technology to streamline operations. As I was establishing a name in this market, I was being recognized as a T-Shirtwala. I started focusing upon every department in depth. I planned to incorporate a dedicated system for barcoding, billing, etc within the store. Gradually, as we were getting results, we decided to take one more franchise of a fashion brand that was dealing in casual clothes for men, women and kids. Unfortunately, that company shut down after some time, so we could not get the stock from that company.

Thereafter, I started purchasing readymade garments from Delhi Tank road. I often visited Delhi every month to check out and purchase new stuff. Gradually, I noticed that this was similarly done by many other players wherein they were open to negotiations done by the customers.. Foreseeing that this concept wont work for long, I gradually converted that store into a multi-brand T-Shirt store. It took me considerable time to check, examine, filter and finalize a few great T-Shirt brands which were excellent in terms of quality, texture and value for money.

Finally, after putting in 15 years of research, efforts and money, we succeeded in creating an exclusive store for T-Shirts by the name 'The T-Shirt Shop'. The brand emerged as a one stop shop for all kinds of T-Shirts. It was born as India's first multi-brand specialized T-Shirt Shop.

Over time, we expanded to multiple outlets and began offering franchises, becoming India's first multi-brand specialized T-Shirt shop. My entrepreneurial journey has taught me the importance of resilience, determination, and adaptability in the business world. Every new venture taught me new skills and helped me in becoming better.

As a budding entrepreneur, I believe that my story can inspire others to pursue their dreams, take risks, and persevere despite obstacles. Through my experiences, I hope to encourage others to have faith in their abilities and to embrace the power of resilience and determination. I believe that anyone can achieve success if they remain focused, committed, and persistent in the face of adversity.

Who Should Read This Book?

T-Shirts are versatile products that can be dressed up and are a great way to express your personality. But starting a T-Shirt business can be daunting. Where do you start? How do you find the suitable designs? How do you get your T-Shirts into the hands of customers? I never ever wondered that my passion for T-Shirts would lead to a place where I would be writing an exclusive book for people aspiring to be a T-Shirtpreneur. On a broader level, this book is absolutely for those entrepreneurs who are passionate about building a successful retail business. The book has been written in a way that will entice the regular readers as well to at least read this book once. Even if you are willing to take a franchise, then also this book would be a value add for you. So, what is the wait for? Keep going and have a great time reading this creation!

Our Milestones

With immense pride, I would like to take you through our Milestones journey.

2008:

We opened our first Tantra EBO

2010:

We became the distributor and secured the master franchise Offbeat for Rajasthan. This enabled us to expand its product portfolio and cater to a wider audience.

2011:

We opened India's first retail outlet at Jaipur Airport exclusively for T-Shirts

2015:

We founded a new specialized multi brand retail concept called "The T-Shirt Shop."

2018:

We were the first to open exclusive Specialized T-Shirt outlets on Highways and midways.

2019:

We partnered with WYO to start retail outlets named 'The T-Shirt Shop by WYO'. We also opened 22 stores in 8 states within 18 months. Same year, we also became the channel partner for Casablanca, one of the leading plain T-Shirt manufacturers in India

2022:

We were invited as one of the panel speakers by Ginesys One in their retail conclave

Decoding The Challenges Faced By Small Fashion Retailers

During this journey of establishing the T-Shirt Shop, I realized that small fashion retailers face several challenges when it comes to managing day-to-day operations. I worked upon the key challenges that are or were being faced by small fashion retailers. Apart from the obvious reason being competition, I deconstructed the entire situation and found several other challenges that I have penned down below. So, if you are one of those small fashion retailers who is finding it challenging to scale up your business setup, then read and understand every point mentioned below.

1. **Competition from larger retailers:** The first challenge is undoubtedly 'Competition'. After speaking with around 75+ small retailers, I understood one point that they get direct and stiff competition from large retailers which eventually is impacting their sales and profitability. Moreover, the marketing budgets and resources get impacted at the same time. In such a scenario, it's time to discover your differentiating elements; basically what sets you apart or different from large retailers. Try offering unique products and experiences to your customer to compete and scale

your business effectively. On the other hand, do not get demotivated with the present retails on e-commerce platforms. Though they are offering their products at lowest prices, it is best to carve your own strategy to meet the needs of your target audience.

2. **Use of Technology to Streamline Operations:** The power of Technology cannot be measured in today's time. Its reach and impact is beyond one's control. However, today, small fashion retailers are being resistant to change by not embracing and implementing new technology solutions and processes in their business model. On the other hand, large retailers are utilizing technology to the fullest and gaining benefits manifold; which in a way is one of the biggest challenges being faced by small fashion retailers. It is high time that small retailers should have in-house expertise to identify the right technology solutions, implement them and manage them continuously. Implementation of technology in your business process will streamline operations and will help in scaling the business.

3. **Inventory Management:** Inventory Management is also one of the challenges being faced by small fashion retailers. When it comes to meeting customer demands, it is equally important to keep a track of one's inventory; ensure that there is appropriate stock in place. Though, inventory management can be a

time-consuming and challenging task, yet implement the best systems and practices in place. This will especially help in dealing with multiple suppliers and styles.

4. **Cash Flow Management:** Cash Flow plays a vital role in day to day management and operations of a business. This is one of the challenges faced by small fashion retailers. As a business owner, ensure to have enough cash on hand to pay off expenditures pertaining to stock/inventory, rent, miscellaneous expenses and other expenditures. During slower sales periods, it is very challenging to manage cash flow.

5. **Visual Merchandising:** Large fashion retailers have an edge over small retailers for obvious reasons. One such aspect that aids them is visual merchandising. Thus, as a small fashion retailer, embracing visual merchandising can completely change your business dynamics. By creating an attractive and engaging in-store experience showcasing your products and brand, you can definitely carve your place in this competitive and cluttered market.

6. **Staff Management:** With limited resources, funds and ad-hoc sales/profitability patterns, small fashion retailers prefer to keep very limited staff. But, eventually, down the line, it makes it very challenging to manage day-to-day operations. As a result, both the customer

and sales get impacted. Hence, as a business owner, it is essential to manage your staff appropriately. When I say manage your staff, it means that right from hiring the right talent, scheduling the staff, imparting regular training, & monitoring their daily performance to retaining them, needs to be done with precision and accuracy.

7. **Marketing and Advertising:** As a small fashion retailer, the marketing budgets are very tight and limited. As a result, they keep on struggling with positioning or placing their brand right in front of their potential customers. Also, finding cost-effective ways to promote their business and attract new customers can be challenging. Thus, it is best to devise strategies or actions that can help small retailers in marketing and advertising their brand in least available funds.

8. **Health Regimen:** Not only small fashion retailers, but other retailers too face health challenges due to the nature of their work. With endless stress pointers and the biggest challenge of meeting the sales target, adversely impacts both mental and physical well-being of a person. So, as a business owner or even if you are an individual, I would emphasize one thing, that 'Nothing is more important than your health'. Prioritize your physical and mental health to manage or run your business effectively by maintaining a healthy work-life balance.

The above-mentioned challenges are the ones that I have discovered over the time. To overcome these challenges, small fashion retailers can consider implementing technology solutions to streamline operations, improve inventory management, control cash flows and enhance the customer experience. Additionally, seeking guidance from business advisors or mentors can help them navigate the challenges of managing a small fashion retail business.

Deconstructing The Retail Code

Introduction to Retail Management

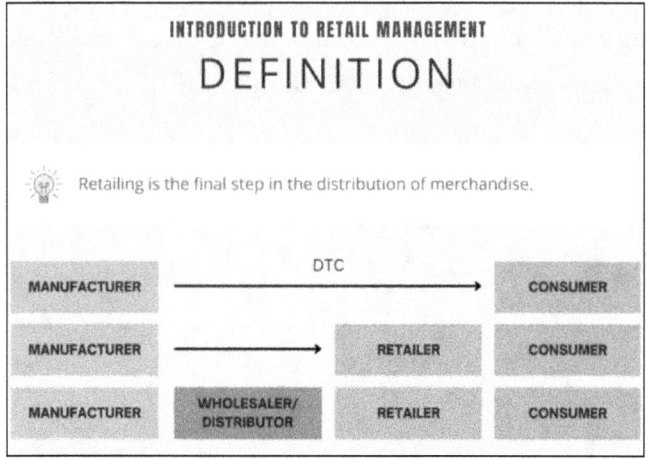

Retail Business Model Canvas

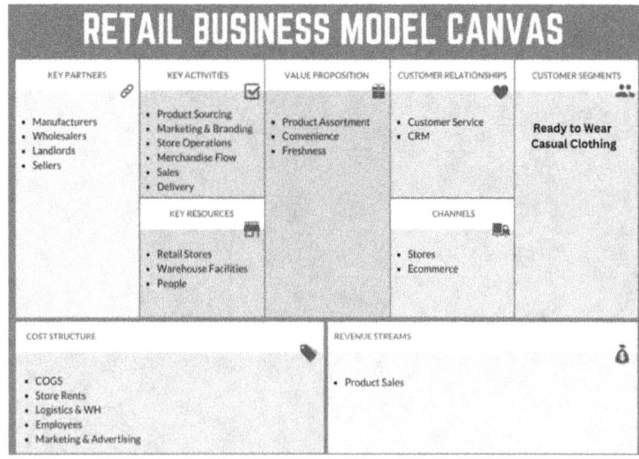

Retail Mathematics

Gross Margin (%) = (Sales - Cost) ÷ Sales x 100
Markdown (%) = (Original Price - Sale Price) ÷ Original Price x 100
Markup (%) = (Sale Price - Cost Price) ÷ Cost Price x 100
EBITDA = Net Profit + Interest + Taxes + Depreciation + Amortization
Net Profit Margin (%) = (Net Income ÷ Revenue) x 100
Inventory Turnover = COGS ÷ Average Inventory at Cost
Sell Thru (%) = No. of Units Sold ÷ No. of Units Received x 100
ATV = Sales ÷ No. of Transactions
Conversion = No. of Transactions ÷ Traffic x 100

Future of T-Shirt Industry

Overview

Consumers' wardrobes, in India and across the world, are undergoing a distinct shift – from formal clothing to a greater preference for trendy and casual attire. The following feature takes a look at the Indian market for one of the most commonly used apparel categories over the world – T-Shirts.

T-Shirts are not just a fashion essential – they are a medium for expression and an ageless insignia of the young and the young at heart. What evolved from undergarments have today become a ubiquitous piece of clothing across the globe. It's easy to wear, comfortable, stylish, finds space at almost every occasion and hence everybody has one.

The Indian Market

According to the latest reports from India's leading management consulting firm Technopak Advisors Pvt. Ltd the size of the T-Shirt market in India is estimated to be at Rs 23,211 crore. This is further expected to grow at a promising CAGR of 10 percent over the next decade to reach Rs 61,954 crore by 2027.

According to industry reports, in the present scenario, men's wear holds a key share in the market, followed by women's wear and kidswear. At the same time, the women's segment is registering a faster growth that experts attribute to the comparatively lower base of market size and increasing acceptance of casual clothing among women. Overall, the Indian Market is accelerating towards a positive growth trend in all the three T-Shirt categories namely, men, women and kids.

The Growth Drivers

Like elsewhere in the world, the Indian consumers' distinct shift from formal clothing to trendy and casual attire has provided a boost to the T-Shirt market in the country. Comfort characteristics, easy-care properties, affordability, easy- design options and a casual look are the major driving forces propelling the T- shirt market in India. Although the youth of the country still remain the core consumer base, the salient features of this comfy apparel has helped the demand trickle down to all age groups today. Increasing acceptance of T-Shirts by corporates is one of the most noticeable trends. Even professional services companies, over the years, have relaxed their dress code to allow business casual t-shirts to the office. Initially, T-Shirts were being permitted only on Fridays, but with time, such relaxations have been extended to all working days by some companies and are expected to be followed by many others.

Price Points

Easy availability and lower price of T-Shirts are also one of the main reasons for this segment's popularity. Prices in this category vary from t-shirt to t-shirt and category to category including, round neck t-shirts, polo tees, mercerized cotton tees, organic tees, etc. So the cost of making the product tends to be changing its price. As customers demand more casual wear than other categories, it impacts the price movement too.

In organized retail the majority of T-Shirts are priced between Rs 299 to Rs 999, mid-premium brands have t-shirts priced from Rs 1,099 to Rs 2,299. And for premium brands the price could be from Rs 2,599 and can go up to Rs 5,999 and in some cases can be even more.

Preferred Fabrics

The rise of the modern discerning consumer has compelled t-shirt manufacturers and retailers to explore various dimensions of product innovation primarily related to product design, colour selection options and fabric combinations. Although fabric preferences in t-shirts vary with season, cotton and cotton blends are by far the most popular fabrics. The most common type of fabric used to make t-shirts is cotton. There are different types of cotton also out there for use. Combed cotton, organic cotton, pima cotton, slub cotton and few more. With the increased awareness about the gym and workout wear, the Athleisure line which is made with polyester as a key fabric as well as elastane in it is gaining popularity in the market. Also gaining momentum are man-made fabrics that offer stretch and fluidity. Cotton will always be popular in India. But now you also see a lot of blends such as cotton/poly, cotton modal, cotton spandex, etc. People like garments that are comfortable and stretchable.

Top Trends

When it comes to clothing, T-Shirts enjoy a special place in our wardrobe. It is one particular outfit that is loved by almost one and all. Since the 50s, T-Shirts have come a long way in terms of popularity, styles, patterns, size, fit, occasion, etc. Today, trends in T-Shirts are also changing faster than seasons. Today, Tees are no longer the same basic outfits. They have drastically evolved in a way that today T-Shirts define your attitudes, style and beliefs. There are different styles and patterns of T-Shirts such as Basic T-Shirts, Solid color T-Shirts, Cew Neck T-Shirts, Short and Long sleeves T-Shirts, Graphic T-Shirts, printed T-Shirts, etc. When it comes to neck, almost every style is in demand be it polo neck, V-neck, round neck, collared, etc. The fit also changes such as straight fit, boyfriend T-Shirts, plus size, dry fit, athleisure, sportswear and many others.

In the last few years, slogan tees have captured a huge chunk of the market. A noticeable trend has created waves in the fashion world and is experiencing a surging demand for t-shirts. Longline tees, sporty look, slogan tees, abstract graphics and placement tees are the current top trends and designs in knitted t- shirts.

Amidst this wide variety, printed t-shirts have managed to grab the attention of Indian consumers the most. Buyers, especially the youth and millennials have started preferring print and design of T-Shirts. There is an altogether different trend being set for funny quotes, famous dialogues from various popular soap operas, sarcastic statements, reflecting tourist locations, mythological stories, cartoon characters, famous personalities and attractive slogans. Demand for t-shirts with embellishments, neon colors, etc., have gained a lot of attention too among the youth in recent times. Tees designed with movie characters and superhero prints are also having a major trend moment.

Conclusion

Irrespective of being a highly fragmented market, the T-Shirt market is witnessing increasing brand awareness among the Indian youth. This brand awareness is expected to drive the penetration of t-shirt brands into smaller cities and rural India. The customer today is quite educated and is aware of his likes, dislikes and preferences. With thorough clarity, he knows what he wants. Hence, as a business owner, it is essential to have utmost clarity and knowledge about your potential customer. The t-shirt market in India is flourishing and is expected to register bolstered growth in the coming years.

Profitability Hacks For Aspiring And Established T-Shirtpreneurs

Dear Readers, we are now at the most awaited section of this book. Being a passionate T-Shirtpreneur does sound glamorous but honestly the journey was no less than struggles, immense learning and experiences. After decoding the challenges that are faced by small retailers, I discovered certain profitability hacks that will not only accelerate your progress but will also help you in being an established T-Shirtpreneur. So, what are you waiting for? Dive deep and discover my 7 game changing profitability hacks that are particularly meant for aspiring and established T-Shirtpreneur.

Hack #1

Understanding Your Competition in Retail

Competition is one such aspect which cannot be controlled but can be won if appropriate strategies are implemented. So, if you are a small fashion retailer, fret no more. Competing with large brands can be challenging, but it is not impossible. I am hereby listing a few strategies that can help you in competing.

1. **Focus on your niche:** The first and foremost hack towards understanding your competition is 'focusing on your niche'. Large brands or companies focus upon attracting a broad audience; which ideally means that they are not catering to a particular niche. But, as a small retailer, you can identify your niche and master that zone by focusing on it. You can design and provide high-quality products and services that cater to that niche. By doing so, you will not only stand out from the competition but you will also establish a unique identity in the eyes of your customers. Your niche could be anything; right from sustainable fashion, vintage clothing, bottom wear, shirts to jeans.

   How we implemented: We cracked this hack way back before launching 'The T-Shirt Shop'. We brainstormed and then decided our niche. That's when we started focusing on our niche and launched a specialized retail brand called 'The T-Shirt Shop.

2. **Offer exceptional customer service:** If you are a small fashion retailer, then definitely this will be an advantage for you. You can provide personalized customer service to your customers and meet their needs and requirements. But, before that, it is very essential to take out time and understand the problem areas, need gaps, requirements and preferences of your customers. After this, you can design and develop a personalized customer strategy and provide them with the required

product or service. This will build customer loyalty and the likelihood to return and recommend your store to others.

How we implemented: We understand the importance of this golden nugget hack. Thus, we understood the requirements of our customers and started offering customized services. We are also equipped with a complete in-house printing unit through which we give any kind of prints and customization to our customers as per their requirement.

3. **Create a unique brand identity:** Undoubtedly, large brands always have an upper hand due to the availability of resources to invest in. Usually, large retailers invest in branding and thus enjoy heavy footfall and viewerships. So, does that mean it is impossible for small fashion retailers? Not at all. If you are a small fashion retailer, you can still implement or take certain moves or steps that can help you in creating a unique brand identity.

How we implemented: To create a unique brand identity for 'The T-Shirt shop', we positioned ourselves as a one stop shop for all kinds of T-Shirts needed for all the age groups and genders. We crafted theme based T-Shirt and expressive T-Shirts with different creative captions tapping different occasions and moods of customers.

4. **Collaborate with other Brands and businesses:** Collaboration is the need of the hour. Collaborating and partnering with other businesses and brands can help in expanding your reach and in offering unique products and services. Keep a tap on growing brands and businesses that have followers in huge numbers. Collaborate with them and promote and market each other's products and services.

   How we implemented: We collaborated with WYO brand i.e. Wear Your Opinion brand. Thereafter, we opened stores with the name 'The T-Shirt Shop by WYO' across India.

5. **Curate your product offering:** Once your niche and target audience is identified, you can then curate a product offering that caters to the preferences and needs of your target customer. You can come up with a mix of your brand products and products from other brands that align well with your brand niche and values.

   How we implemented: We implemented this hack by curating around 10 different brands. Thereafter, we created unique multi-brand outlets that are offering all the varieties of T-Shirts from fashion to basics.

So, if you are planning to compete with larger brands, then simply implement the above mentioned hacks and grow your business exponentially.

Hack #2

Auto-Piloting The Operations

As a business owner, it is very essential to auto-pilot your business operations or else you will end up in a messed up business ecosystem. So, if you own a fashion outlet, then this hack will help you in auto-piloting the business operations. I have been fortunate enough to learn and understand the power of implementing this hack from one of my mentors Mr. Rahul Jain who is one of the leading business coaches in India.

Hence, find some of the ways which can aid in automating your Inventory in Fashion Retail business operations.

1. Implement Inventory Management System or IMS system: Create a pull based IMS system for purchases. Basically, you should buy only what sells.

2. Initially, order only a few pieces of each item or design especially when a new season starts.

3. Thereafter, re-order only those pieces that were sold in the first 20 to 30 days. Apart from this, simply move and place the remaining pieces towards the discount shelf. Ensure that those pieces do not block the main shelf.

4. Now, reduce the rates of these pieces till the extent that the value of the product is equal to the price. This will eventually boost sales of those pieces.

5. In case, still there are certain pieces that are not moving at all then sell them at any price. Do not wait.

6. Balance out the stock in 80/20 ratio. Refrain from keeping pieces or stock whose sale is 20% I.e. lowest.

7. Sales Pro Tip: Offering too many choices or options to your customers/clients will not be a better move. It is a proven formula i.e. Less Choice = More Sales

Hack #3

Using Technology to Auto Pilot the Operations

Technology plays a vital role in scaling your business as well as saves time and effort. We are hereby listing tips of using technology to auto pilot the operations.

1. **Implement Point of Sale (POS) System:** As a business owner and a small fashion retailer, it is essential to understand the essence of Technology in streamlining business operations. Get a high quality POS system or point of sale system that can aid in automating your cash management, sales tracking and inventory management. With this, you can invest your energies on other areas of your business. In a way, it is one of the apt hacks to save your time and effort.

   How we implemented: Initially, when we started our first store, we didn't have any proper systems in place for billing. So, we used to provide invoices to our customers in a hard copy format. We were not having barcodes on our products. This took a lot of time to complete the entire billing process. This made me realize that if I continue this further, then I would not be able to scale my business. This way, I will be sitting at the cash counter and store to keep a watch on cash and stock. Then, one of my mentors suggested that I implement POS systems in place. So, initially, we introduced offline POS for our store and then later migrated to cloud POS. With this, we succeeded in scaling our business as well as providing franchisees of our concept.

2. **Implementing Daily Sales Report:** A daily sales report (DSR) is one of the mandatory inclusions for getting updated about the sales on a daily basis. It is essential to get this report filled by store managers on a day to day basis to track the sales and then compare it for further analysis.

3. **Petty Cash Management:** Petty cash management can turn to be a tedious task if management is done manually. Today, due to technological advancements, one can find a series of Cash Book apps that are perfect for day to day petty expenditure. So, we also installed a cash book app that helped us in petty cash management. This app gives a complete view with a voucher attached of the expenses made by the store at any given point of time. Apart from this, one should maintain a Google Sheet as well.

4. **Leave Approval system:** Google Forms if used in the right way can prove to be beneficial for business. There should be a proper leave approval system in place to record the leaves of employees across departments.

5. **Making online presence without much technical know how:** Our organization has been able to create an online presence with the help of the Quicksell application, which has proven to be a reliable and user-friendly tool for catalog management across both B2C and B2B sectors. In addition to cataloging, we have also utilized the application's website builder feature to create our company websites with utmost ease and convenience. The Quicksell application has greatly facilitated our digital marketing efforts, enabling us to showcase our products and services to a wider audience without the need for extensive technical expertise.

6. **Using CRM tool:** Reminding customers to come back if they have not visited the store for long can be done through a proper CRM tool. Sending them birthday wishes, anniversary wishes and running loyalty programs can be good to keep the customer reminded about your brand and keep the connection on.

Hack #4

Automate Warehouse Operation for Retail Fulfillment

As a business owner, it is important for you to automate your Warehouse Operation process for Retail fulfillment in order to transform your business towards profitability. But how? Read further and discover.

1. **Utilization of process management sheets or tools:** With technological advancements in place, there is an availability of several software tools that can aid in streamlining your operations. For example: Maintaining Google Sheets or creating Google Forms can help you in automating your daily activity checklists. In fact, as it is a Cloud product, you can share it within employees as we as access it on the go. Similarly, there are different tools such as Biometrics or Geolocation attendance system, Inventory management sheet (IMS) to keep track of stock levels, task automation software to automate your task delegations, FMS sheet to automate the flow of goods receiving and delivery.

   How we implemented: We understood the importance of this hack when we were juggling with our stocks. We had certain products that were evergreen and were in high demand. So, we identified those products which should be always available at our outlets. We decided that such products should be always in stock or never out of stock or NOS. So, we implemented an IMS wherein we gave an input for the minimum level of stock. It was a mandate to maintain a minimum level of stock at the store. In case, the stock goes below the minimum level, then the software will provide an auto indent which needs to be fulfilled by the warehouse team on immediate basis. By doing this, we ensure to prevent missing out on our sales as well as intend to balance stock levels.

In addition to this, we also set a minimum level of stock in our POS system. This automatically generated the indent for that stock. We maintained flow chart management sheets for timely delivery of goods. Our sheets are properly defined. Every step is defined with the exact turn around time from the previous step. It covers aspects pertaining to 'WHAT has to be done', 'WHO will do it', 'HOW will it be done, WHEN will it be done', etc.

We have also implemented a Task Management Tool that aids us in delegating one time tasks for our team. We also maintain a KRA checklist for keeping a track of the recurring task of each employee.

2. **Training Videos:** Videos are impactful if used in the most effective way. In these progressive times, almost every person today is heading forward to create a Youtube Channel for their target audience. This not only aids in establishing your presence as an expert but it also acts as an effective way to inform and

educate your people. One of the key challenges that business owners face is in training their staff or employees. Right from hiring reliable people to handing over the sales and operations of your outlet is a critical thing. It is essential to train your staff well on customer service, sales, inventory management, and basic store operations so that they can handle routine tasks without your constant supervision.

So, what we did here: We created our Youtube Channel. We shot our videos pertaining to different job roles and tasks in the company. We recorded all our processes in these videos to facilitate an ease for employees to get trained. We uploaded these videos on our Youtube Channel. This has reduced our stress of training the employees on a recurring basis. Rather, this has helped them to get trained easily with proper SOPs. New joinees can view these videos and learn about the entire process.

3. **Monitor Performance Metrics:** You should keep a track of key performance metrics such as sales, inventory turnover, KPI of staff and customer satisfaction to ensure that your outlets are running smoothly. This tracker aids in recording all the data for future analysis. Thus, this data should be analyzed to understand and identify areas that require improvement and make data-driven decisions.

How we implemented: At 'The T-Shirt Shop', we utilize and maintain daily KPI report sheets that are auto generated and are mailed to the respective concerned person. They can check the performance of the store and compare it with previous week, month and with the sales of previous year. We provide a digital bill to the customers on every purchase. They can also provide us with feedback or rating through that digital bill. If the ratings turn out to be low, then it will be escalated directly to the top management to further look into the concerned matter.

4. **Task Automation:** We have implemented two different types of automation in our processes namely, one time task automation and recurring task automation. In one time task automation, there is only one task for which the process is automated. While, in a recurring task automation, there are a series of tasks that occur on a recurring basis. The sheet is automated and is accessible to all the concerned people.

5. **Scoring of the Task:** Scoring system helps the employees in knowing and checking their performance week on week, month on month and year on year. The scores are automatically generated and the report is mailed to the team people.

6. **MIS Reporting:** MIS reporting or Management information system reporting is a critical process in the company. Basically, an MIS Report refers to a report that is prepared for the management of the company based on the data that is collected automatically from different systems within the organization. We, at The T-Shirt Shop have also implemented a MIS reporting system to get access to information pertaining to the people, data, hardware, software and business procedures.

With the help of these strategies, you can make your fashion outlets and warehouse operations run on autopilot mode and free up your time to focus on growing your business.

Hack #5

Monitor your Cash Flow Management

Understanding the essence of cash flow management for a small fashion retailer is a must. If you are running a retail outlet, then this point is right for you. But, before that, let us understand what is Cash Flow Management? In a layman term, cash flow management is tracking the money that is coming in and out of a business. In this process, one needs to monitor, analyze and optimize the net amount of cash receipts - deducting the expenditure.

For this, you need to implement a financial management system. This will help you to track your expenses, revenues and profits. These important details pertaining to cash flow will help you in making informed decisions with respect to inventory, pricing and other elements of running and growing the business.

It is my honor to mention my mentor Mr. Jagmohan Singh, who is one of the leading cash flow experts and coaches in India. I implemented his key learnings in my business model and witnessed a steady growth of my business. Hence, I am hereby sharing a few essential steps that will help you in setting a proper cash flow management system for your business.

1. Pursue a Profit First Principle. Apply this formula, Cost = Revenue - Profit

2. Ensure to pay off all the salaries and wages to your team on a fixed day of month.

3. **Four Bank Accounts:** As a business owner, it is very important to manage and regulate your bank accounts well. Thus, if you are juggling with cash flow management, then open four different bank accounts.

    a. **Inflow:** There is one dedicated account i.e. inflow account wherein the inflow of funds should be deposited. All the incoming payments will flow in this account.

    b. **Payable:** Open a separate Payable account wherein you will initiate all your payments to vendors for goods and services.

    c. **Expenses:** A separate bank account to be maintained for paying expenses such as telephone bills, electricity, salary and other fixed cost expenditures.

    d. **Cash Reserve:** There is a specified percentage of collection that should be transferred to this account. This will act as a Cash Reserve for the company. You should avoid withdrawing money from this account. This account is only for the growing cash reserve of the company. You should deposit 5% to 15% from Inflow every week or 15 days in this account.

4. As a business owner, ensure to make the payment on a periodic basis. You can prefer to keep it either weekly, fortnightly or monthly. Please refrain from keeping it daily. Do not purchase by paying in advance or by paying upfront. Why? Because of the strong credibility and reputation in financial dealing earned by our company. It is ideal to purchase as per PO or purchase order system with a maximum allowed credit period. One should abide by the terms of payment mentioned in the vendor registration form.

5. You should pay your periodic bills such as telephone bills, electricity bills, etc through credit/debit cards of the company. Clear off the credit card dues on time within the immediate month to avoid recurring interest rates and penalties.

6. Create an Expense Purchase Order for recording all the expenditures apart from petty cash and period expenses.

7. Prepare an automation sheet to maintain and record petty cash expenses.

8. Prepare accounts payable aging reports with the help of an accounting software. These reports can be prepared and generated on a periodic basis.

9. Keep a track of the Return on Investments made.

10. Allocate your expenses properly. Never utilize short term money for paying off long term expenditures.

11. Pay your vendors online after uploading payment details on the bank portal.

12. Ensure that you are never out of cash balance. Also, keep a check on the cash balance of six months.

13. Maintain an ideal working capital as per the business model

14. There should not be any policy for providing loans to employees for home or car or motorbike. If there is any requirement, then you can open an Employees Bank account for facilitating all credit facilities directly by the bank.

15. There should be a special voucher system in companies specifically only for the business owner to withdraw money from business.

16. Follow a cash flow model rather than operating from bank balance. Ensure to save and earn money rather than spending it. All the incomes should be accounted for and noted.
17. None of the unauthorized expenses or purchases be made except EPO and PO.
18. Clear your bills in full. Payment of bills before or within the due date increases credibility. Credit is not just money. There is more to it. Credit defines the reliability and confidence that should be preserved and protected.
19. Initially, create reserves as a first cushion and thereafter place credit as a second cushion. It is in those needy hours that we generate and earn more money.
20. Solvency of a company impacts its survival. Solvency of a company depends on making more money than spending it.

By following these steps, you can set up a proper cash flow management system that will help your small fashion retail outlet stay financially healthy and grow over time.

Hack #6

Implementing Visual Merchandising

Being a small fashion retailer has its own set of challenges as well. There might be difficulties and challenges in attracting and retaining customers. Thus, one such hack that could be helpful for your business in this scenario is Visual Merchandising. Visual merchandising can play a crucial role in addressing these challenges by creating an attractive and engaging in-store experience that showcases your products and brand. But, how? We have listed a series of steps that can be useful to small fashion retailers in improvising visual merchandising. Moreover, by implementing visual merchandising, you can emerge to be a self-service store without being fully dependent on sales staff.

They are given below:

1. **Implement a user-friendly store layout:** Design the store in a way that allows customers to easily find what they are looking for without the need for assistance. Organize the products into categories and provide clear signage to guide customers.

2. **Use signage effectively:** Use signs and banners to communicate important information about your products or promotions. Make sure they are easy to read and grab viewers attention.

3. **Provide ample product information:** Make sure your products are well- labeled and provide detailed information such as size, color and materials used. This can help customers make informed purchasing decisions without the need for assistance.

4. **Create a focal point:** Choose one area of your store to feature a standout display, such as a mannequin dressed in your latest collection or a collection of accessories arranged on a unique display fixture. This will draw customers in and create a memorable impression.

5. **Simplify the checkout process:** Implement easy checkout systems that allow customers to pay by any payment mode they want (UPI, card, cash etc). Digital prints of bills is also a good option which can be sent to customers through SMS or whatsapp.

6. **Train staff to be available but not intrusive:** While you may not want to be dependent on sales staff, it's important to have staff available to answer questions and assist with any issues that may arise. However, staff should also be trained to provide customers with space and privacy to browse and make purchases on their own.

Hack #7

Putting Inventory Management At Top Priority

Last, and one of the most important hacks to attain profitability is putting inventory management at top priority. Inventory Management is one particular area wherein there is a lot to juggle with; especially for small fashion retailers. But, appropriate planning and management can help you in handling this area with finesse and ease. As a small fashion retailer, you need to keep a track of stock levels and ensure that most selling items are always in stock. Irrespective of the size of business, it is important to manage your inventory well. So, how is that possible? I have a solution for that.

When we started ' The T-Shirt shop', we too had this trouble dealing with our inventory. So, to simplify this area, we implemented a robust inventory management system that helps in tracking sales, monitoring stock levels and managing returns and exchanges. This will help in ensuring that the store always has the right products in stock, reducing the likelihood of stockouts and optimizing stock levels.

You can refer to some of the steps to manage your inventory effectively:

1. **Analyze sales data:** Review your sales data to identify which products are selling the most and which ones are not. This will help you make informed decisions on which items to keep in stock and which ones to reduce.

2. **Set par levels:** Establish the minimum amount of stock you need to keep on hand at all times. This will help you avoid stockouts and overstocking.

3. **Keeping Proper stock of NOOS:** NOOS stands for "Never Out Of Stock". It is a type of merchandise that is sold and stocked all year round and is not subject to seasonality.

4. **Set up a tracking system:** Use a spreadsheet or inventory management software to keep track of your inventory. Record the name of the item, its cost, the quantity you have in stock and the date you received it.

5. **Consider using a barcode system:** Implementing a barcode system can help you streamline your inventory management process, reduce errors and save time.

6. **Keep track of inventory:** Use an inventory management system to keep track of your inventory levels. This will help you know when to reorder products and ensure that you always have the right amount of stock on hand.

7. **Conduct regular audits:** Conduct regular inventory audits to ensure that your records are accurate and that there are no discrepancies.

8. **Prioritize fast-moving products:** Ensure that you always have enough of the products that sell the most. This will help you avoid lost sales due to stockouts.

9. **Offer promotions:** Offer discounts on slow-moving products to help clear out excess inventory.

10. **Work with suppliers:** Maintain a good relationship with your suppliers to ensure that you receive your orders on time and at the right price.

11. **Optimize your ordering process:** Establish minimum and maximum stock levels for each item to ensure you always have enough inventory on hand. Consider using a just-in-time (JIT) ordering system, where you order new stock only when you need it.

By following these steps, you can effectively manage your inventory in a small fashion retail outlet and ensure that you always have the right amount of stock on hand to meet customer demand.

Working Towards Your Health & Wellness

Till now, we got a detailed understanding about different hacks that will help you in becoming a profitable T-Shirtpreneur. But, amidst all these hacks, strategies, tools, etc, one such thing which is most important is your health.

As a business owner, there are plenty of things to look after. With multiple tasks to handle and at the same time keep the business growing is not as easy as it sounds. Hence, in this journey, it is your health that needs to be taken care of. Irrespective of being mental health, physical health or emotional health, one should take regular measures to nourish and nurture your physical and mental well being. As a retail owner, it's important to prioritize your physical and mental well-being in order to effectively manage your business and maintain a healthy work-life balance. Here are some tips to help you achieve healthy mental well-being.

Tips to maintain your Physical and Mental Well-being:

1. **Prioritize self-care:** We often miss practicing self-care. When it comes to self-care, it does not restrict to simple grooming or wearing good clothes. There is something more to it. Self-care refers to those measures that you

take for your mental and physical regimen. Take out some time for yourself and dedicate particular hours of your day for yourself. Pick up a workout routine, meditation or simply go for a swim. This will channelize your happy hormones and help you in rejuvenating your physical and mental health.

2. **Work life balance:** This is an equally important element - learn to set boundaries. In order to balance your work life and personal life, it is important to schedule your day in a way that even if you disconnect from any one element, it does not get hampered. This will also open up doors for welcoming new opportunities in your life.

3. **Practice stress management techniques:** Stress is a very natural element in our life that cannot be eliminated due to obvious reasons but it can be moderated in a way that it does not impact you within. By practicing stress management techniques, you can relax yourself from within and welcome new perspectives in life. Adopt practices such as yoga, deep breathing or any mental well being program which will help will prevent you from stress and anxiety.

4. **Connect and socialize:** Man is a social animal. Simply doing your business will not lead you anywhere. You need to connect and network with others to grow yourself exponentially. You can join and be a part of

a local business group where you can connect with like minded people. Attend networking events and broaden your business circle by connecting with other business owners.

5. **Focus on the positives:** As Robin Sharma says, 'An entrepreneurial journey is like seasons. You should embrace it well.' Yes, unlike seasons, as a business owner too you will experience highs and lows in your business. Amidst all the chaos, the one who survives it well emerges to be a leader in himself. But how can one achieve this? Well, the answer is by being positive. Rather than counting the negatives, direct your focus towards the positives in your entrepreneurial journey. Give importance to positives and celebrate every small or big success or progress that you have achieved.

6. **Give importance to Sleep schedule:** We have been hearing this proverb all our life, 'Early to bed, early to rise, makes a man healthy, wealthy and wise.' But, how many of us religiously follow this? Well, sleep is one of the most important elements that is often overlooked. Our mind and body require a minimum 7 to 8 hours of sound sleep to rebuild and rejuvenate. Appropriate sleep flushes out the toxins and reduces stress and anxiety. It imparts energy and fuel to the body to function our best the following day.

My Recommendations For Wellness Courses

Well, I am an ardent fitness lover and believe in taking utmost care of my mental and physical health. Therefore, apart from working out, I have also experienced certain wellness courses that helped me grow and nurture as a person internally. Read more and know about a few of my recommended programs for Wellness.

A) Happiness program of Art of Living

The Art of Living needs no introduction. A mission run by Sri Sri Ravi Sankar, is an ideal destination to discover a newer you. Their 3 days Happiness Program is a uniquely designed program that will help you in being happy from within, calmer, lighter and will give you clarity in your life.

What are the benefits of doing this program?

The following are some of the major benefits that you will embrace:

1. **Enhanced and increased Stamina:** The 3 day course will help you in overcoming fatigue and tiredness. You will experience a drastic shift in your energy levels and help in boosting your stamina. This will also prepare

you to do your day to day activities with complete energy without getting tired or drained.

2. **Eliminates and relieves depression, anxiety and stress:** The techniques and exercises done under this 3 day program will help in reducing your stress, depression and anxiety even during difficult times.

3. **Boosts health and immunity:** While pursuing this program, you will discover some highly effective and backed with research techniques that will boost your immune function, reduce the risk of heart disease and channelise your overall energy levels.

4. **Develop capabilities to deal with your mental situation:** This program will teach you ways with which you can manage your mind and control rather than it being vice versa. The techniques will help you in dealing situations wisely and calmly with the help of your own emotions and thoughts with wisdom and awareness.

B) Advance Meditation Program (AMC)

Apart from the above mentioned program, you can also go for the Advanced Meditation Program in the Art of Living. Basically, this is a residential program which takes you further into your spiritual practices and more advanced breathing techniques that can be easily learnt and practiced alone.

What are the benefits of doing this program?

The following are some of the major benefits that you will embrace:

1. **Explore meaningful silences:** This program is an advanced level workshop that takes you deeper into the world of guided meditation. It will enable you to dig beyond your active mind and experience tranquility. You will achieve and experience a renewed vitality.

2. **Experience deep meditations:** This workshop includes Gurudev Sri Sri Ravi Shankar's guided meditations which are called "Hollow and Empty". It is a central part of this program. This meditation will help you in settling into a deep rest.

3. **Build and increase immunity:** The detailed meditation exercises will sooth your nervous system and will channelise the smooth flow of energy through the body. This will boost and increase your immunity.

4. **Eliminates emotional stress:** The meditative practices in this workshop will help you in touching the deepest layers of your stress and eliminate them. You will feel relieved, de-stressed and reconnect with a newer rejuvenated version of yourself.

5. **Experience higher energy levels:** The life force or prana in your mind and body increases and enhances with the meditative practises done in this programme. The higher the prana, the calmer and positive is your mind.

6. **Unlock new levels of creativity:** It is in deep silence that you can unlock and unleash new doors of opportunities and creativity. This advanced meditation program will take you in an altogether different state of deep rest wherein you will be disconnected from the mental chatter. Here, you will discover your skills and talents.

I have pursued these programs and have experienced all the benefits too. Truly, it was a life changing experience for me.

Recommendation For Meal Routine For Retailers

As a retailer, you will often face this challenge of balancing your meals along with your work. We often have this tendency to prioritize our work over our meals. Though, it might not show you its results in a short term course, but it will gradually impact your health in the long run.

So, it is important to set a proper meal schedule irrespective of being challenging. As work schedules vary and are demanding at the same time, it is important to prioritize it above all. After experiencing and knowing about its importance, I am hereby listing some recommendations for Meal Routine for Retailers that are practical to follow.

1. **Draft a clear plan beforehand:** Planning is the key to achieving your goals. It is important to plan your schedule well in advance and create or block specific times for your meals in your calendar. Do keep your work commitments schedule aligned with your meal planner. This will allow you to have a relaxed meal time and you will also eat mindfully. This will keep you energetic throughout the day.

2. **Pick your healthy options well:** While planning your meal, consider only those food items that are nutritious and are rich in minerals and vitamins. The sugar count should be low with no unsaturated and saturated fats. Try to include only home cooked food that will give you a clean eating experience.

3. **Take adequate breaks:** A break truly sorts everything. Taking regular breaks throughout the day can help you stay refreshed and avoid burnout. Try to take a break every few hours to stretch, take a walk, or simply rest and recharge.

4. **Refrain from having your meals at your workstation:** Work while you work and eat while you eat. This is also applicable for the space where you are doing that particular thing. So, eat your meals at a dedicated place only. Do not consume food or meals at your desk. This will prevent you from mindless and over-eating. Discover a right spot in your office or near your workplace where you can calmly have your meal.

5. **Consume meals at fixed times:** As a retailer you will definitely struggle with this but you have to work towards achieving it. As per Ayurveda, you should consume your food items at a fixed time. Consuming food at ad-hoc times, might lead to health issues. Hence, breakfast, lunch and dinner should be done at fixed time only. Carry your lunch and dinner at your shop and have it on time.

I have seen that while hustling, we often keep our meals and other important things at bay. But, the ground reality is that we are actually keeping our healthy life and future at bay. Thus, as a special mention, I have hereby included certain ways and measures that can be easily adopted and implemented to live a healthy and prosperous life.

Testimonials

1. **Harsh (Krishna enterprises) - An Accountant turned into a T-Shirtpreneur:** Harsh used to work as an accountant in Sweet Ginger. Being an accountant by profession, he was good at calculating the return on investment and financial viability of any business. He explored a few options before opting for the franchise of The T-Shirt Shop. He found out that The T-Shirt Shop is a concept which is quite easy to manage promising a good return on investment. Also, the company supported him in stock, inventory and billing in a fair and transparent manner. He took the franchise of The T-Shirt shop and is running the shop successfully and profitably.

2. **Honey Motwani (Dhruv Enterprises) - Salesman at medical shop turned into a T-Shirtpreneur:** Honey used to work at a medical shop as a salesman. Unfortunately, he lost his job during covid. Then he decided to take the franchise of The T-Shirt Shop. He is running it profitably and successfully -with full auto-pilot system. Now, he has made this shop as a passive income stream for him. He realized that since the company system is auto-pilot and shops can be

managed by hiring staff so he joined a job also and has parallelly made this shop as a passive income for him and for his family. He does not have to visit the shop on a daily basis.

3. **Rajat - (Shotia Fashions):** Rajat is a young guy who was looking for a business opportunity. His parents are into the auto parts business but Rajat wanted to do something on his own which he can build from starting. He visited The T-Shirt Shop in Jaipur and really got impressed with the concept. He took the decision to start the same concept in his hometown where he felt that this concept would work great. He took the franchise of The T-Shirt Shop and is running it successfully now in Sikar. Within 1 year of operations, he found himself financially settled and decided to get married.

4. **Heeralal Soni - (Priyanshi Enterprises) - Salesman at Garment shop turned into a T-Shirtpreneur:** Heeralal Soni started his career by working as a sales executive at a fashion retail shop. Then, he joined 'The T-Shirt shop' as a salesman. After working for a few years, he was promoted to Store manager and then he started managing the store. During his journey he found out that The T-Shirt Shop is growing and really easy to manage with systems in place. His parents were into property business which was really affected post covid. He started looking for some business opportunities so

Testimonials

that he can help his family. He took the franchise of The T-Shirt Shop in 2020. With his dedication and support from the company, today he is running a successful franchise of The T-Shirt Shop. He has also bought his own house after that.

Conclusion

The learnings never conclude, rather they are the gateway to new opportunities and learnings. Through this book, I have made an effort to educate the target readers about some of the effective profitability hacks to become a successful T-Shirtpreneur. Still, I believe there is a lot more to what I have mentioned. Yet, I would love to summarize few golden key takeaways

1. Focus on your niche
2. Understand the importance of automation in business
3. Implementation of technology to auto pilot business operations
4. Importance of monitoring your cash flow management
5. Implementation of visual merchandising process for Retail outlets
6. Considering Inventory Management at Top Priority

Heartfelt Gratitude For Readers

So, as I end my book here, I would like to thank all my readers for taking out the time from their busy schedule to read this book. It gives me a sense of pride for having my book in your reading space.

I tried my best to make this book a value add in your life. I strive to pen down the learnings that I gained from my experience in this book. I hope that I succeeded in doing so. Do consider sharing this book further to help me create an impact in the life of my readers.

Let's Connect...

If you feel that there is more to learn and you are seeking additional guidance beyond the material provided in this book, please don't hesitate to contact me at shankar@thetshirtshop.in. I am available to answer any questions you may have and provide further insights on the topic. Additionally, I offer 1-on-1 consultation calls for those who would like more personalized attention and advice. Thank you for your interest in expanding your knowledge and skills.

Book a 1 on 1 call with me.

https://bit.ly/meetingwithshankar

You can follow The T-Shirt shop on:

www.instagram.com/thetshirtshopindia/

Let's Connect...

◼ www.facebook.com/ttss16

⬛ www.linkedin.com/company/the-t-shirt-shop/

▶ youtube.com/channel/UCTsH0lxP2WEwsM8ZjgCN_zg

Join our T-Shirtpreneur Club

The T-Shirtpreneur Club is a new community created by Shankar Hemrajani that is dedicated to empowering new age entrepreneurs who are interested in starting and growing their own T-Shirt businesses. Whether you' are a seasoned entrepreneur or just getting started, the T-Shirtpreneur Club offers a welcoming and supportive environment where you can learn, grow, and succeed in the exciting world of T-Shirt business. This community is designed to provide members with the necessary tools, resources, and support to help them succeed in this competitive industry. Members will also have the opportunity to connect and network with like-minded individuals who share their passion for T-Shirtpreneurship.

www.facebook.com/groups/tshirtpreneurclub/?mibextid=NSMWBT

www.ingramcontent.com/pod-product-compliance
Lightning Source LLC
LaVergne TN
LVHW010605070526
838199LV00063BA/5083